T.M. Cooks is the pen name of the following collaborative writing team. The contributors are;

- Ella Louise Harrison
- Lexi Mai Smart
- Roxy Louise Smart Hughes

The project was overseen by Yvonne Skipper.

The group cheerfully acknowledges the wonderful help given by:

- Jane Thorne
- Claire Hollins
- Richard Seymour
- Michael Fay
- Phill Dann
- Daniel Holland
- Elizabeth Platt

- Tilli Smith

- Izzy Jordan

- Zena Cooke

- Everyone at the Donna Louise Children's Hospice

-

-

-

It's been a wonderful opportunity, and everyone involved has been filled with incredible knowledge and enthusiasm.

The group started to plan out their novel at 10.00 on Monday 20th August 2018 and completed their last proof reading at 12.30 on Friday 24th January 2018.

We are incredibly proud to state that every every idea, every chapter and yes, every mistake, is their own work.

We are sure you will agree that this is an incredible achievement. It has been a true delight and privilege to see this group of young people turn into professional novelists in front of our very eyes.

Were is She?

T. M. Cooks

Contents

1 The Tidying Begins   7

2 Behind the Closed Door   13

3 Meeting the Royal Family   19

4 Meet the Talking Animals   23

5 The Greeting of the Dark Master   29

6 The Capture of a Sister   37

7	Bella needs help	41
8	Turning Bella	45
9	The Finding	47
10	The Plot	51
11	Into the Lair	55
12	The Red Eyes	61
13	The Appearance of Mum	65
14	The Secret Past	69
15	The Powerful Stone	75
16	The Big Battle	79
17	A Million Pieces	85
18	Growing Up	91

Chapter 1

The Tidying Begins

Location: At Home

Time: Morning

It was about nine o'clock in the morning and Alexa had just been told to clean her room but she didn't want to. "I don't want to" she shouted at her mum and then stormed out to the back garden. Mum didn't look so happy. She then came back in the room and Mum then asked her again to clean her room and again she told her Mum she didn't want to. "Don't be so gobby!" Her Mum replied back to her. Alexa said " I am not being gobby, I just don't want to clean my room."

"Well your sister is always cleaning that room so why can't you do it for a change?"

Just then Bella came downstairs from listening to her classical music. "I heard shouting. What is going on?" she asked her Mum.

"Well your silly twin won't go and clean the room for a change, " she said. Bella then said she would go and tidy her room. Alexa was told by her mum that she was not having her pocket money that week for not doing the bedroom. Bella had just gone upstairs to clean the room. In a flash she was back downstairs because she had cleaned the room already.

Alexa went upstairs. After about half an hour later she came downstairs. Mum had asked her what she had been doing but she just ignored her. " I said what have you been doing!" Mum said to Alexa as she still ignored her Mother. So Mum sent Bella upstairs to look.

Bella went to look upstairs. She came back down looking a bit upset. "What is wrong?" Her mum asked. " You're a brat I can't believe you messed the room up!" She screamed at her twin.

"I'm sorry not sorry" Alexa replied with a smirk on her face. "Well you're always so responsible, learn to have fun" Alexa said.

As it was getting too much, Alexa tried to run out of the house but instead she tripped over her sister's book. She tried to look angry but instead she had to laugh. Just after, she ran as fast as she could out of the house down the dirty street. Then she stopped and sat down on the floor and started crying. Bella had just seen something on the floor, at first it was a speck, then a dot, then as she got closer a blob, then a girl, then she finally realised it was Alexa, so she ran over to comfort her. The girls then got off the floor and started walking down the street as they made things better with each other.

Chapter 2

Behind the Closed Door

Location: Enchanted Shop

Time: Morning

The twins walked down the street to

find an old rusty and dusty shop. It seemed that no one had gone into the shop in years. In the windows of the shop there were dusty and very old ornaments. The shop was so old that it was even crumbling as the sun shone. On the top of the shop there was a sign that was rustily hanging off and said that people could go in.

Alexa said "The shop looks cool, maybe we should go and check it out."

On the door it said open/closed. They pulled the old door that was covered in scratches. Every time it moved it creaked. The sound went through Bella and Alexa.

They walked into the rusty dusty old shop. It smelled, because it had not been cleaned in years. They could smell dust and it made them cough. They could hear water dripping from a damp leak in the ceiling. The walls were mouldy. On all the shelves there were either broken ornaments or cracked ornaments with dust all over.

They found a door when they walked to the back of the shop. They opened the door to find themselves in a jungle, they were shocked to find a jungle. It was an amazing jungle.

There were lush green leaves everywhere. It was raining but the air was warm and it was very damp. They started sweating so their vision was murky. It was so nice to be in a magical place where all the animals could talk to each other.

They looked behind them and they couldn't find the door so Bella and Alexa thought that it was covered in all the branches and trees so they looked to find the door. They didn't find the door as it had disappeared into the day. They screamed very loud, so all the rainforest could hear them. They needed someone to help them get home. They were scared in case they were going to get eaten by predators.

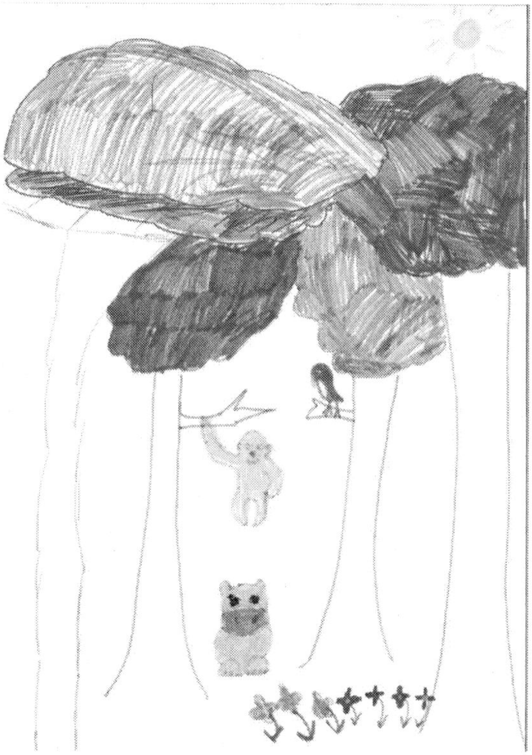

Chapter 3

Meeting the Royal Family

Location: Jungle

Time: Lunch time

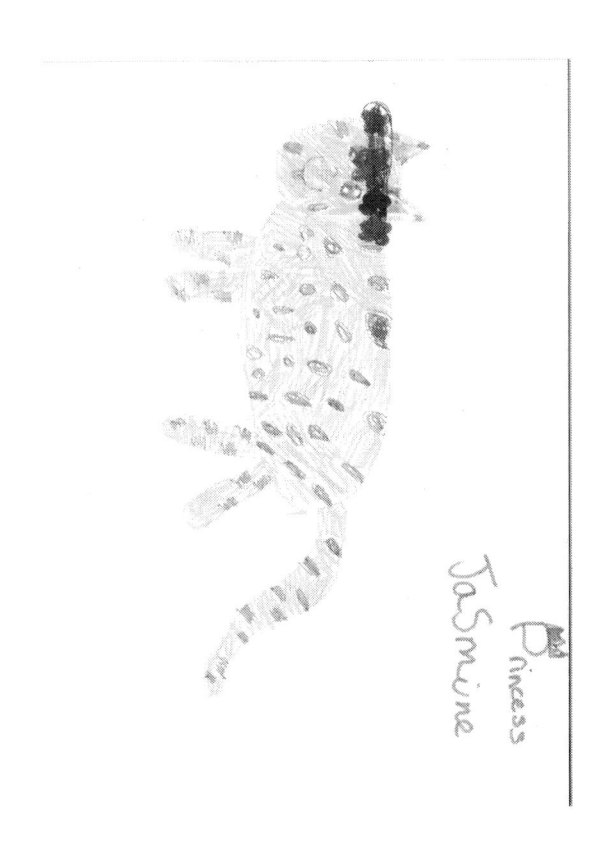

They saw a spotted jaguar and she was called Jasmine. She said she was the daughter of the King and Queen of the jungle.

She said come and meet my family in the palace. Jasmine the jaguar went over to the twins. "Hello my name is Jasmine Jaguar."

"Hi. Our names are Alexa and Bella."

"Let's go and show you around the jungle, where to go and not to go" Jasmine said to the twins. Bella said "how will we get home because the door has gone so we can't get back home." Jasmine said that they didn't need to worry about going back.

They walked into the gold and white beautiful palace with 10 bedrooms and balconies with all of them, to go and see Jasmine's parents, who were the King and Queen of the jungle and then they went to meet the Good Crew.

Chapter 4

Meet the Talking Animals

```
Location: Jungle

Time: Dinner Time
```

Bella, Alexa and Jasmine walked out

of the beautiful palace. Jasmine said "I want you to meet my friends, let's go to the kitchens so you can meet our chef, he makes tasty lasagne." Bella and Alexa both said at the same time "GREAT let's go!" So off they went to the palace's kitchen.

They walked into the kitchen they saw loads and loads of shining pots and pans. It smelt like a horrible breath. It also smelt like something tasty was cooking. I could hear a bit of hippo hop music. As we turned round the corner I saw a dancing hippo in a stainless white chef hat and apron wiggling his bottom.

Jasmine jaguar then tapped the dancing hippo on the back and said "Hi Hassan. I would like you to meet my new friends Alexa and Bella."

In the twins' heads they were thinking

that the hippo was very big and very grey and that he had a very big bottom. "Hi I'm Hassan the hippo. Nice to meet you." he said.

" Hello we are Alexa and Bella. Nice to meet you too."

Jasmine then said to Hassan that they were sorry but they had to go, and they walked out of the kitchen. They then walked out of the palace and Jasmine said to the twins "Shall we go and meet my another friend Peri the parrot at the park in the middle of the jungle?" They all walked to the park and saw a brightly coloured parrot swinging on the monkey bars.

Jasmine tapped the swinging parrot on the wing and said " Hi Peri, are you ok? Meet my new friends Alexa and Bella, " Jasmine said. Peri said " Hi. I'm Peri.

Nice to meet you too." In Bella and Alexa's heads they were thinking wow, how beautiful. They were thinking that because he was brightly coloured.

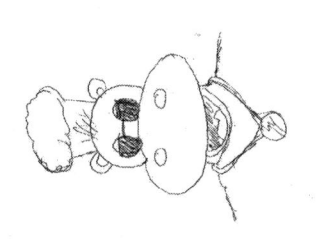

Chapter 5

The Greeting of the Dark Master

Location:Meeting Room

Time: Middle of the Day

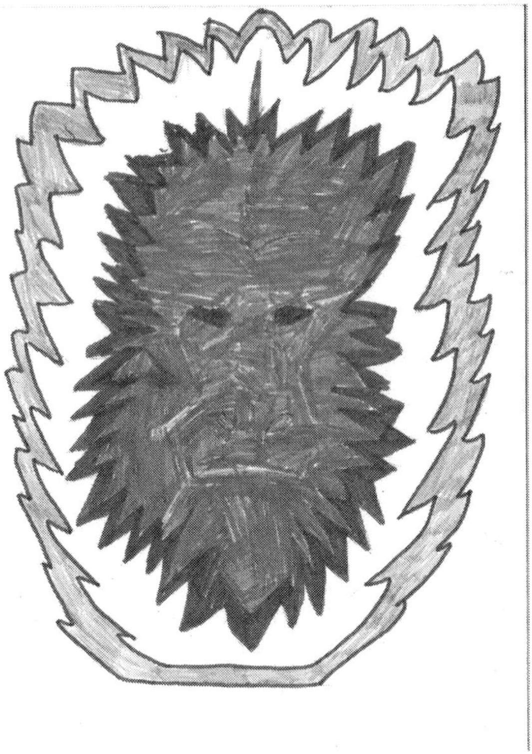

The Dark Master (gorilla) called a meeting for the Bad Crew to discuss something about the stone to make him powerful so that he could rule the jungle that his Dad wanted him to rule.

"I need the stones to be powerful and take over the kingdom so I can be King of the jungle

forever and that I don't mess it up for me or you, or we will be out of the Crew forever."

"The stone isn't complete yet. I need the last three pieces from the lockets and put them together to be powerful and rule the kingdom. So let's go and capture the people with the lockets. The leopard said "How do we capture them if we don't know who they are or how to get to them?"

"Spilky can set up a web to catch them all so I can rule the jungle."

"When I'm King I will have a much better place to live, by putting the King and

Queen and her daughter in jail and the Good Crew on our side, so they will turn bad so we don't have a single person who is good in the jungle".

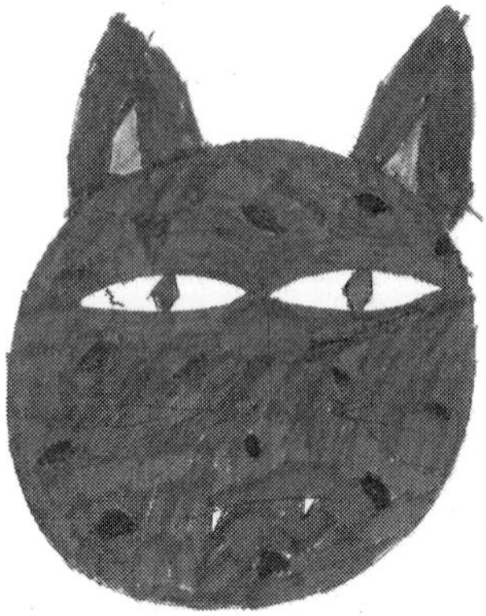

SPIKEY

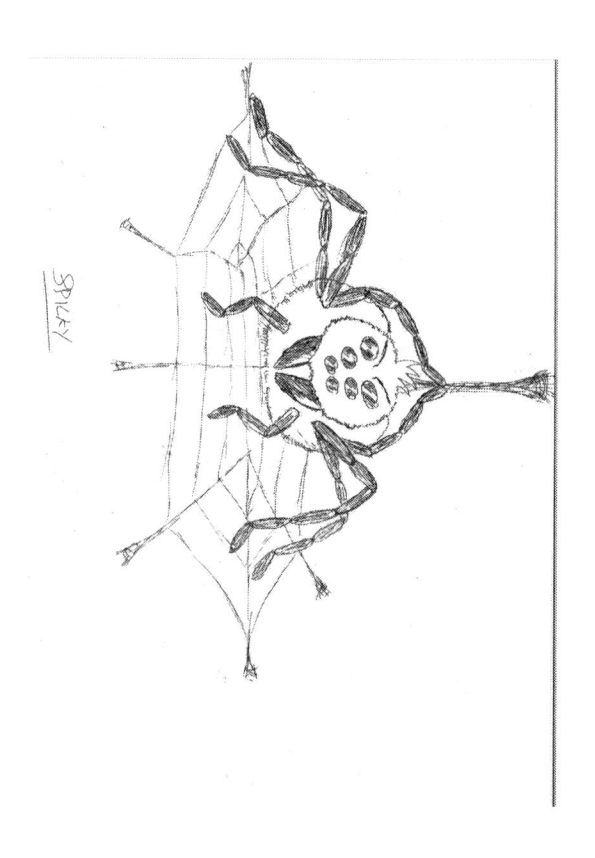

Chapter 6

The Capture of a Sister

Location: In the tunnel and jungle

Time: Middle of the day

"I think the jungle is amazing. It's full

of wonderful things, seeing there are green leaves, trees, flowers and the wonderful sun."

All of a sudden she saw a bird. It was beautiful. She followed it away from the others. Just then she saw a tunnel.

The bird went into a tunnel. It was full of black leaves twigs and sticks. It also smelt of rotted bodies and she saw a human body to the side of her, she turned her head very slowly then she screamed "ahhhhhhh!!!!!!!!!!!!!!!!".

She followed the bird to the end of the tunnel. She carried on walking until she came to a door. The door was dirty, rusty and dilapidated.

Bella found the courage to open the door to the Bad Crew's retreat. On the other side of the door the Bad Crew were waiting to catch Bella. When Bella opened the door, a super big spider's web caught her. Bella gave a long, loud, piercing cry. The gorilla got the leopard to stop her from getting out of the spider's web. The leopard accidentally scratched her cheek.

The snake showed his fangs and let off a venom into the air but the Bad Crew didn't pass out from the venom because they weren't scared of snakes. But Bella passed out because she was agitated. The snake then heaved her into the wooden cage.

Chapter 7

Bella needs help

Location: Gorilla's Lair

Time: 2pm

The cage that Bella was in was dark, damp, deep, smelly, mouldy and you could hear the dripping sounds of the flowing water. Bella felt extremely scared because she couldn't find a way out until she heard the guards coming towards the big old wooden cage. Bella couldn't find the key to escape.

She failed to find the key so she thought of other ways to get out, like digging herself out. That was a fail, so she thought of climbing the wall, but that was also a fail. She thought of looking for a secret passage. She found one but it was locked! Bella felt upset because all of the attempts were a big, big fail. She wanted her Mum.

Bella wanted her Mum because she was scared and afraid. Bella opened up her locket and held the picture of her mum and gave the locket a rub and said "Mum I really need you, I am ever so scared."

Back in the real world, Mum was doing the dishes. Then all of a sudden, her locket started to flash as if something was wrong. Then she heard the voice of Bella saying that she was scared and needed her mother. So she dropped all of the dishes, some even smashed. She ran out of the house as quick as she could and noticed the old shop that the twins had noticed. So she walked in and disappeared...

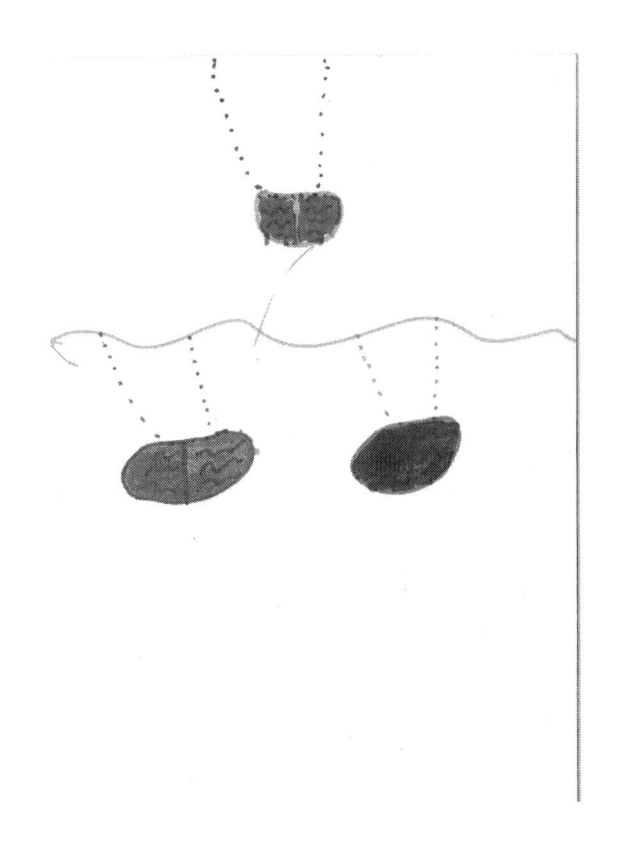

Chapter 8

Turning Bella

Location:Dark Woods

Time: 3pm

The gorilla comes down the ladders to talk with Bella. The gorilla said "The only way I will let you be free is if you come on the Bad Crew." Bella said "I will not come on the Bad Crew ever". The gorilla climbed up the ladder to the other side of the cage and shook his head and said "you're not going anywhere".

Gorilla said "I know about the the stone in your locket, your twin sister and her locket as well". Bella said "How do you know about the locket? You will not have the stone from mine and Alexa's so just give up now".

"You will have no control over our lockets so leave the stone as you will never be King anyway."

The gorilla said "never because I NEED to be King, I have been waiting for this day to come always".

Chapter 9

The Finding

```
Location: In the Jungle

Time:4pm
```

Alexa was so worried about her sister and wished that she was with her because they had such good fun when they were together. She thought "I am going to try and find her myself".

Alexa wandered off...

Alexa went to find her sister. She walked through the dark jungle looking for her sister. She felt very upset. When she was looking she found a dark small tunnel. She could hear noise from the tunnel. It was Bella's voice.

Alexa went through the tunnel to find Bella, in a wooden cage. Alexa went up to the cage and said "I will get you out soon".

Bella said "Thank you for finding me, I have missed you".

Alexa said "I will go and get help from the Good Crew."

Alexa sprinted back through the tunnel to arrange a plan for Bella .

Chapter 10

The Plot

```
Location: Palace

Time:4:30pm
```

The animals were thinking of a plan to get Bella out of the massive wooden cage. Jasmine the Jaguar said "We shall have a meeting later on at the palace in the dining room, everyone is invited apart from Peri because he can't keep a secret and he is too chatty. If Peri comes to the meeting, she would tell the baddies the plan".

Alexa said to Jaguar Jasmine that they should have a meeting about saving Bella. They invited the other animals. "Hey Hassan, you are invited to our meeting at my palace at 4pm about rescuing Bella and we need you because you are big and strong. Hey Alexa, you're invited to our meeting."

Peri, you're not invited to the meeting because you come up with terrible ideas and we will tell you the plan afterwards.

Everyone went back to the palace and had a brilliant meeting.

The plan is to fight, get the key, set her free and go home and tell Mum everything.

Peri got upset because all of the others wouldn't let him go to the royal meeting. So, he went off to the Bad Crew and told them the plan. He went to the Bad Crew's den.

"The Good Crew are going to try and fight you so you need to get ready for battle. They want to set Bella free" Peri said.

"Ok we will go and prepare, they are going to lose and we are going to win. And I will get all the pieces of the emerald stone like I deserve!" the Dark Master said.

"Spilky, go and make one of your enormous webs. Scar go and sparkle and sharpen your teeth. Woah I'm a poet and I did not know it! Rattle, go and venom your sharp teeth. Monkey go and eat your bananas and put your peels on the floor. Sheera go and fluff your fur and sharpen your sword.

Speed, go and get your bow and arrows ready for the battle. We will be ready for them."

Chapter 11

Into the Lair

```
Location:The Lair

Time:Tea time
```

The Good Crew stormed into the lair, looking for the Bad Crew. They went to free Bella from the Bad Crew, Hassan said

"To free Bella we have to fight to set her free." So then the Bad Crew and the Good Crew fought .

Jasmine took on the gorilla and they fought. Jasmine wanted to get the key to set Bella free from the gorilla. Jasmine swiped the gorilla with her claws, the gorilla was getting angry because he was being scratched by the jaguar. The gorilla jumped, up and down and he banged his fists around. The jaguar moved very quickly to move out of the way.

In the jungle the leopard, Scar, was trying to tease the hippopotamus by jumping onto the hippo's back and pushing him into the water. The hippo was trying to jump out and was screaming for someone to help him. Alexa came and helped the hippo out of the water but the leopard was still trying to hurt him with his claws. Alexa started to fight with the leopard but realised that he was too strong so she gave up. She went to help Jasmine with the gorilla. Hassan the hippo went to the tree to hide from the leopard.

The parrot, Peri, was flying about trying to get away from the army and catchers that were trying to catch him. Peri the parrot was flapping his wings very hard to get away faster. The monkey was swinging from tree to tree in the jungle. The spider was making his spider web very quickly to catch Peri the parrot. The rattlesnake was hiding in a tree catch the parrot if he stopped.

Peri went to the gorilla to say "Can I join your crew?"

The gorilla said "Yes you can join our

crew, we need a lot of help".

The gorilla shouted to everybody "The parrot is on our side!"

Jasmine was shocked and Alexa said "why has the parrot joined the Bad Crew ?"

The parrot said "because you didn't invite me to the meeting and I didn't feel part of the Good Crew".

Alexa slipped through between the gorilla and the jaguar to get to Bella. Alexa said " I WILL GET YOU OUT SOON DON'T WORRY!!!"

Bella said "I TRUST YOU" . Then Alexa was fighting the gorilla to help Jasmine the jaguar. The Dark Master was getting resentful, swinging his arms around and roaring .

Sherare the lion was fighting the hippo,

who doesn't like fighting and was trying to run away. But lion likes fighting a lot and won't let the hippo escape the fight. Then Jasmine shouted "LION LOOK OUT!!!!!!!!!!!!!!!" lion looked around to see what was happening and hippo punched the lion in the face and then ran off.

Jasmine thought of a way to get the key out of the Dark Master's hand. She remembered that he was very ticklish, she said "look over there, Bella is escaping, " and when he looked, she tickled his tummy and he dropped the key. Alexa picked it up and dropped it down the cage to Bella. Bella caught the key and climbed up the ladder with the key to open the door to the cage .

After Bella got out of the cage, Alexa said " COME ON GUYS, BELLA IS FREE."

They ran rapidly through the tunnel to get to the other side and blocked the tunnel with a hefty stone .

Chapter 12

The Red Eyes

```
Location Gorilla Lair

Time: After the escape
```

The Dark Master was furiously angry at everyone for letting the children escape from the wooden cage. He was fuming that he couldn't get all of the pieces of stone from the lockets the children had. The Dark Master's eyes were flashing red, orange because he didn't get what he wanted. When the gorilla got a little bit angry his eyes, turned light red and when he became

absolutely angry his eyes turned dark red. Also when he got angry he banged his chest for a very long time.

The Dark Master wasn't upset or angry with the leopard as he was his special helper. Scar the leopard has a scar underneath his right eye, his fur is black and red. His age was 41. His favourite food was arms from little children and other animals. When he ate little children's arms the blood dripped out of his mouth and you could hear the crunch of the bone.

When the others saw the leopard doing

all of his dripping and crunching they felt sick from all of the disgustment.

The Dark Master was saying to the leopard that we will get them next time if they don't think of another plan between them. I am going to punish all of the others by locking them in the wooden cage for the night, because they let the children go and didn't catch them. You don't have to go in because you tried to stop them from escaping, so nice work Scar.

Chapter 13

The Appearance of Mum

```
Location: Jungle

Time:6pm
```

Bella and Alexa were in the jungle and wished they had their Mum.

"I wish Mum was here, because I miss her, " said Bella.

"Me too, " said Alexa. "I miss her, too."

They both grabbed their lockets, rubbed them and said, "I wish you were here, Mother."

There was a wind. All the trees were swaying from side to side. The leaves made a rustling noise. Bella and Alexa knew their Mum was about to appear. They felt really excited. And they felt a bit nervous in case it all went wrong. Suddenly there was a flash and a streak of lightning coming from the sky. They jumped back as if they were about to get struck by lightning. Alexa said that she was scared in case it's not Mum. And then all of a sudden their Mum appeared. "I'm here. What's wrong?"

"This morning I was rude and ignorant. I need to learn my responsibilities. Mum, I am sorry for being gobby this morning."

"It's fine, but don't do it again, " said their Mum.

"We need you to help us in the fight to get the stone back."

"I'll join, but Alexa you have to clean your room when you get back."

"I will Mum, I promise."

"Well, are you in?" asked Bella.

"I'm in, " Mum said.

Chapter 14

The Secret Past

```
Location: Jungle

Time: In the Past
```

In the past, Mum was the ruler of the jungle. Samaira (Mum) made sure everyone was safe and she told the servants to check on the royal family to see if they needed anything.

She had a telescope so she could see the whole of the jungle so Samaira(Mum) could make sure that everyone was safe.

Mum was caring and respectful of everybody, she was little, had dark brown hair, multi-coloured eyes and she also liked to wear dresses and skirts.

She wanted to ensure that nobody would do bad things so she created a stone which would help them control the other people in the jungle so they too are good, kind and caring.

Then she cast a spell on the gorilla who was called Bob and the stone, then the spell went wrong and he became mean and wanted to rule the jungle for himself. Then he became known as the Dark Master.

Mum tried to get the stick which had the jewel on, so she could stop the spell from getting worse and make sure he wasn't the ruler of the jungle. She sneaked into his bedroom at night and she tried to steal the stone, but she couldn't steal the whole magical stone, so she stole three small pieces. He couldn't become the King, without all the pieces together.

Mum couldn't make him good again.

The Dark Master got a Crew of animals together which had a spider called Spilky, a monkey called Shiver and a rattlesnake called Rattle. They were the Catchers', they caught animals and humans to eat. He also had a tiger called Speed, a lion called Sherare, and a leopard called Scar who was his second in command and they were the army and helped to keep the Dark

Master safe.

Mum couldn't get the stone because it was so well protected by the Crew.

Mum took the pieces into the real world to keep them safe from the Dark Master.

Mum had twins named Alexa and Bella.

She wants to keep them safe from the jungle and so keeps them away from the magic shop.

She didn't forgive herself for what she had done because she felt guilty.

She is worried about the Gorilla and other animals in case they do bad things and she worries about the effects on the Queen and King.

If she smashed the stone, the spell will be broken and the gorilla and the Crew will turn good forever.

Mum said "I hope that the jungle is safe

and I can break the spell one day soon, so everything will go away and it will all be sorted.

I have the other pieces safe so that the gorilla can't become King of the jungle.

She says "That is a good thing."

Chapter 15

The Powerful Stone

Location: Jungle

Time:Sun Down

The Gorilla calls his crew for a meeting, to think of a plan to help him get all of the pieces to the stone. The last pieces are in

Alexa and her Mum's locket. "At Least I have Bella's piece of the locket, so I can become King if i get the rest, Whoooooohohohohoho!!!

In the meeting they described what the stone looked like. The stone colour was beautiful turquoise and it had glitter all over it. When the light was shining, beaming on it, it turned into an emerald colour, the stone was in the shape of a diamond and it glistened like an actual diamond.

Chapter 16

The Big Battle

```
Location: The Lair

Time: 8pm
```

The Good Animals were all struggling to walk through the big, green forest to go to the gorilla's den because it was a very long walk. It took thirty minutes. It was boiling hot. They were sweating and they were ready to pass out. In the silence of the day they arrived at the scary gorilla's underground tunnel.

They ran in screaming and shouting, ready to fight. The gorilla was on his throne eating his dinner, which was mouldy lasagne. All of a sudden he heard a whispering noise coming from the underground tunnel.

"Let's FIGHT in the underground tunnel, " said the good animals.

The gorilla dropped his food and ran to the fighting room in a flash. The fighting room had a tub of knives and swords, ten shields, a throne, a punching bag and a chain hanging from the ceiling. The tunnel emerged into the fighting room. There was a big, chained metal door in the floor.

SMASH the door slammed open and all the Good Animals came running out of it. They all got their swords out. There were punches and kicks and guts and glory. The fat gorilla got off his throne and kicked the parrot and knocked him flying.

On the other side of the river the hippo was scared, standing there shivering because he was scared to get into the water. But he wanted to save the jungle and be the hero he wanted to be. He had to try and face his fears. SPLASH! He panicked. He felt like he was going to drown. He tried to swim but has he got the hang of it? Mabe. Yes! He's got the hang of it! He swam until he got to the other side. He jumped out of the water with a thud.

"I'm not longer afraid of water! I am over that!" he shouted.

The hippo came running in with the speed of joy and jumped on the Bad Crew. All that was left was the baddest of them all. The Good Crew all fought the gorilla.

"No, I surrender! Please don't hurt me!" the gorilla screamed in anger.

"Okay but give us the stone, " the Good Crew said.

"No I will never give you the stone even if you try!"

They carried on fighting. There were more punches, guts and glory!

Hassan the hippo ran and jumped on the gorilla. The gorilla fell to the ground. The hippo sat on the gorilla's belly and knocked his teeth out.

"I think I have dislocated my shoulder, " said the gorilla.

.

"No one says they THINK they have dislocated their shoulder. They just say I'VE DISLOCATED MY SHOULDER!!!"'

All the animals laughed.

"We've defeated him!" said the hippopotamus.

"Now you need to go on a hunt for the stone, " said Mum.

They all walked out of the room.

Chapter 17

A Million Pieces

```
Location: Jungle

Time: Midnight
```

Alexa, Bella and Mum are all at the dark, dirty and extremely smelly gorilla den and are trying to get the stone.

They need to get the stone because she needs to make things right.

The stone is emerald green and is the size of a football. If you have all of the stone you would be able to take over the jungle.

They need to smash the stone. The twins go behind the gorilla to see the rest of the stone in the gorilla's back pocket on his trousers. With a flash they steal the stone from the angry gorillas pocket.

"Mum we have stolen the stone and the gorilla didn't even notice!" the twins said whilst running like a flash down the tunnel.

" Well done girls you're the best. I would never have been able to do what you have just done!" Mum said looking and sounding amazed.

" how shall we break the stone ?" Alexa asked Bella.

" we should throw it at the wall!" Bella replied.

" it would probably go through the wall but let's give it a try!" Alexa replied.

So then they threw the stone at the dirty and sticky wall.

Guess what happened next... the stone SMASHED into a million and one pieces with a flash of green light. It blinded them all.

Just at that moment, the big gorilla's eyes went from red to indigo and violet. He then went up to the twins' mother and said "I apologise for all the mess I have caused."

Mum said "Well I am glad you have apologised but I'm even happier that you have turned good again."

They then shook hands and hugged.

From their sleep the rest of the Bad Crew wake and feel a bit confused because they feel really strange and they don't know why.

The Bad Crew had now turned good and had no memory of the bad times at all, they had no idea what was going on or had just happened.

They can remember being good but they can't remember anything at all about being bad.

"You were bad, ' said the mother.

"Well I apologise, ' they said.

Chapter 18

Growing Up

```
Location:At home
```

```
Time:Morning
```

Alexa had to tidy her room and she did because she had learnt respect and manners. She also earned her pocket money back. After she put all the toys books and paper away and she hoovered the room. Her mum was very proud. But you will never guess what her twin sister was doing whilst she did this...

She was listening to her favourite classical music. She felt really relaxed because she did not have to do anything. She felt like the room was so tidy she had just been saved from Trampville.

Mum was so happy as she was watching her daughters grow up together very nicely in peace. Alexa had learned to have respect and take responsibility. Bella had learned to relax and play. Mum was very proud to see what she saw now and that they had taken good care of each other in the jungle. Mum was glad she had her daughters to help her along the way.

Later on, at tea time, they were all sitting at the table eating their dinner and the twins were being playful with each other and cat fighting with their hands. They were all very happy and lived happily ever after. *THE END*

Our Authors

Roxy Louise Smart Hughes

Hello my name is Roxy. I am eight years old. I love Big Writes. My favourite thing to do is gymnastics. My character is the Dark Master and he is a mean character in the story and the story comes to life. It only took us a week to write this book! As well there were only three people writing the book. That made me feel quite happy because the book is finished. I really hope you enjoy reading my book. So enjoy reading my book today!

Ella Louise Harrison

My name is Ella, I am 11 years old. I have written a book in a week with only three people! I like to play my clarinet and do art. My character is Bella, she is kind, she does as she is told and she is bubbly and is just like me in real life. I feel happy that I have achieved something like this. Hope you enjoy reading this book!

Lexi Mai Smart

Hi my name is Lexi and I am 10 years old. I love maths but after writing this book I think English is the best. Me and two other people wrote this book together just in a week. My character in the book is

Alexa me and her are so much alike. I also have a twin in real life and her name is Demi. I really enjoyed writing this book because I got to know some people who I didn't know before. It was a great experience and I think everyone is going to enjoy this book. I hope you enjoy reading this book!

Printed in Great Britain
by Amazon